CW00400162

The Mini 'How To' Guide to Retirement

by

Genevieve Desiree

THE 'HOW TO' GUIDE OF RETIREMENT

First published 2020

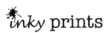
inky prints

DEDICATION

For my dad, the person who's taught me the meaning
and value of hard work and who has truly earned to live
life to the full in his retirement.

Happy retirement Dad!

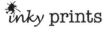

Table of Contents

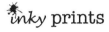

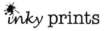

FOREWORD

Retirement is something often seen from different perspectives. Is it a great new adventure or a necessary next step in life? Is it something to be anticipated in excitement or something to be dreaded with dismay? Is it a discovery of one's true self or a loss of one's routine and structured lifestyle?

However you view retirement is entirely up to you however this book offers you a few things to do, a few reasons to retire, and some witty quotes and views on retirement that you can take forward with you on your path towards becoming a true retiree!

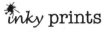

101 things to do when you retire

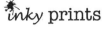

101 THINGS: THE SHORTENED VERSION:

1. Sewing
2. Cross-stitch
3. Crochet
4. Knitting
5. Painting
6. Drawing
7. Origami
8. Napkin folding
9. Towel folding
10. DIY project
11. Learn an instrument
12. Learn a new language
13. Complete an online course
14. Learn some sign language
15. Learn how to juggle
16. Learn how to shuffle
17. Learn how to tie all of the basic eight knots
18. Learn how to read a map
19. Learn how to touch-type
20. Learn the Morse code
21. Grow your own vegetables
22. Create a herb garden
23. Grow a seed from scratch
24. Create a rock garden

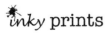

25. Build and grow a greenhouse

26. Take a pottery class!

27. Try windsurfing

28. Or just plain surfing (!)

29. Go to a dance class

30. Get creative with a cookery class

31. Experiment in a cocktail-making or mixology or even wine-tasting class

32. Go to a chocolate-making class

33. Go to a life-drawing class

34. Get stretchy and flexy and go to a Pilates or yoga class

35. And relax with a meditation class

36. Camping

37. Walking / hiking

38. Complete a sporting challenge

39. Take up a new sport

40. Join a local gym

41. Swim, sauna, and steam at a local leisure centre

42. Experiment with open-water swimming

43. Go on a cycle ride

44. Ski through the winter months

45. Or snowboard

Make some...

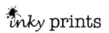

46. Plum and ginger jam

47. Basic blackberry jam

48. Mama's marmalade

49. Simple strawberry jam

50. Cox's apple chutney

51. Mincemeat

52. Lemon curd

53. Apple sauce

54. Tomato relish

55. Peanut butter

56. Volunteer somewhere

57. Do something for charity

58. Fill a shoebox for Operation Christmas Child

59. Do a good deed for someone who is homeless

60. Complete a fundraiser

61. Join a book club

62. Join the WI

63. Join a local community society

64. Form a dining club with friends

65. Join a social club

66. Recreate a favourite childhood

67. Try to cook a new dish.

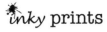

68. Cook an exotic dish from a foreign country that you've always wanted to go to….

69. Bake some bread from scratch

70. Make some pastry from scratch

71. Take a mid-week mini-break

72. Visit the place that you went to on your favourite childhood holiday

73. Visit somewhere you've always dreamed of going

74. Visit a new country

75. Visit a new continent

76. Take a scenic bus ride or train ride

77. Take a boating holiday.

78. Take a break in the sunshine

79. Take a wintry break.

80. Take a city break to a capital city that you haven't yet visited.

81. Re-read a favourite books series

82. Re-watch a series of movies

83. Watch an entire box set

84. Learn a new word from the dictionary every day for a week

85. Read the newspaper with a nice cup of tea or coffee and a biscuit of your choice

86. Sort through all your old photos

87. While you're sorting out… sort out all your clothes

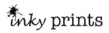 inky prints

88. Polish your shoes

89. Have a spring clean

90. Play a board game

91. Host a Summer-time BBQ (events to host)

92. Have a night in with friends

93. Go to a family party

94. Organise a surprise party

95. Invite your neighbours around for drinks

96. Enjoy an afternoon tea somewhere nice (experiences to enjoy)

97. Treat yourself to a three-course meal

98. Go to the top of a tall building and see the view

99. Watch a show at the theatre

100. Have an indulgent spa day

101. And finally ... put your feet up and relax – you've earned it!

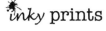

10 WAYS TO…GET CREATING

Often, people put off being creating, fearing that they'll 'do it wrong' or 'mess up'. But, truthfully, being creative can never be wrong, can never be messed up. It all relies on your imagination and your vision for your creation. So, what can you create?

1. Sew it - learn how to sew and stitch up something new – whether that's by following a pattern or just 'winging it'.
2. Cross-stitch – it's easy to find patterns online, or buy a small kit with all the right embroidery threads making it easy for you to pick up and try.
3. Crochet – have you ever tried to create something from wool? With a few simple crocheting techniques, you could create a scarf, or hat for the coming winter. If you enjoy it and keep practising, these could also be great, and thoughtful, Christmas presents for family and friends!

 inky prints

4. Knit – or, if crochet isn't your thing, knitting could be a fun alternative. Also working with wool to create woollen goods such as scarves and hats.

5. Make a painting – whether you've done painting before or whether it's entirely new, get some large paper or a canvas and some paints and create something new.

6. Draw something – if paints aren't your thing, you could try pencils by putting your arty attempts to try sketching. Whether it's an online tutorial that you can follow, or a step-by-step guide book to drawing something, or freestyle and freehand, or copying another artists' work or drawing still life… there's so much you can create with only a pencil at your fingertips!

7. Fold it – origami uses the simple, single staple of paper. Tutorials to create anything, from waterlilies to butterflies, from swans to sunglasses, are available online or in origami books and sets.

8. Fold it, again – the host-with-the-most, or hostest-with-the-mostest, has elegantly folded napkins to adorn their table so why not learn and practice a few simple napkin folds for your next dinner guests?!

9. Fold it, thrice (third time lucky!) – again, something else that goes above and beyond the role of an

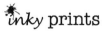

average host / hostess is folded towels. So, while you're. upping your offer to host with folded napkins, why not learn how to fold towels too – something like a cute towel monkey or dog is easy to create and can make your guests feel that 'extra' bit welcome.

10. DIY – do it yourself, whether it's hanging up a picture that has been waiting for it's hook for a while, or something more advanced, such as redoing the bathroom – get stuck in and do it yourself!

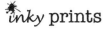 inky prints

Learning can be something that we dismiss as being for children, for school, for education. But we are never finished with our learning in life. Sometimes it is lessons in life that we gain, other times it is new knowledge, techniques, or tools that we train in.

No matter what age, no matter what interests you, learning is a part of life. So, now that you've got the time to dedicate to learning something new, why not try a few of the following…?

1. "If music be the food of *life*, play on…"[1] – take up a new, or old, musical instrument and learn a new piece – or even how to play it from the very beginning. It could be a simple instrument such as the record, or if you've been yearning to play the piano, or guitar, or drums, since childhood but have never had the chance, why not change that and try it now!?

2. "A different language is a different vision of life…"[2] – can you speak another language,

---

[1] Adapted from William Shakespeare's *Twelfth Night*

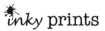 **inky prints**

besides your own native tongue? Offering a new insight into life, another language can break down barriers you didn't know existed and offer you a new outlook and way of living. Deciding to learn a language can be empowering so, with more time to focus and practice, retirement offers the perfect opportunity to learn a new language and widen your own horizons.

3. Online courses are plentiful in topics, and very high in popularity so give your hand at completing an online course. Websites such as *FutureLearn*, or *Reed*, or *The Open University*, offer online, guided, learning paths that allow you to pursue learning anything from psychology to specific historical topics, or Woolf's literature, or even Babylonian mathematics. Take your pick and learn something new from the comfort of your own home.

4. "Only through communication can human life hold meaning"[3]. Not everyone speaks the same language, and some don't speak at all but communicate visually. Widening your capacity to communicate is, arguably, one of the most

---

[2] Federico Fellini
[3] Paolo Freire

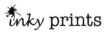 inky prints

meaningful things you can do. Learning sign language – or at least some basics, such as the alphabet, or how to introduce yourself – widens your ability to communicate hugely.

5. Learn how to juggle! Quite often, we juggle multiple things at one time, throughout our lives: whether it's children, or family and friends, or work / life / exercising / social… the list goes on. But how about physical, literal, *actual* juggling? Why not embrace the fun of the circus and try to juggle for real!

6. While you're practising your physical co-ordination and dexterity, why not learn how to shuffle cards too?! Shuffling is often something not many people can do properly so, with a little bit of spare time, learn a few simple shuffling tricks to impress at your next opportunity of playing cards. And remember, practice makes perfect, so if at first you don't succeed, try again!

7. Learning how to tie the different types of knots is something that most nautically-focused individuals take for granted. Yet do you know the difference between a figure-of-eight knot and a slip knot? And, is there a difference between a square knot and a reef knot? Try learning some of

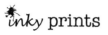 inky prints

the 'knotting' basics by starting with how to tie the initial eight knots, the building blocks of knot-tying.

8. Although the smartphone and increased use and availability of technology such as Googlemaps makes navigation far easier, it's also often useful and actually very interesting to know how to read a physical map. Whether an ordinance survey map is more your style or a roadmap is preferred, grab a map and go exploring, trying to find your way and learning how to read it as you go.

9. Learning how to touch-type is a skill that often comes in handy. Even if you're no longer using a computer for work, try to learn how to touch-type and you'll be surprised at how much time you can save!

10. Although it may never come in handy or be a skill that you ever have to use in practice, learning Morse code can be an interesting exercise so see if you can learn it by dedicating 10-20 minutes a day for a month or two and see how many words you can tap out!

Being outside in nature, being in the wild environment outside, growing and adding to nature, gardening and sewing seeds offers both a psychological outlet for stress and sense of achievement, as well as a practical creation of your own plants, and maybe even produce.

Get out in your garden and try growing a few of these things:

1. Grow your own vegetables – instead of relying on shop-bought produce or frozen veg, try growing your own. Starting with runner beans is often an easy way to get into building up your own vegetable garden and progression to potatoes, turnips, carrots, beetroot… is all attainable and achievable.

2. Herb gardens – easy to sew and grow, especially cress which only needs water (!), herbs not only offer the perfect house plant for those who don't have a garden but also a way of widening your taste palette and cooking horizon as you add new

 inky prints

herbs into your repertoire: coriander, oregano, rosemary… the possibilities are endless!

3. All plants take time to grow, but why not try and plant your very own seedling and watch it grow from scratch. You'll be surprised at how it develops and blossoms over time.

4. If you do have a garden, creating a rock garden can be a nice way of adding something novel or new to its appearance. Easy but also very eye-catching, rock gardens are a nice way of adding variation or differentiation to a simple lawn and are very low-maintenance, generally.

5. Get a greenhouse – greenhouses are great for growing things that need a little more maintenance and care. Dedicate more time and tools to really allowing your crops to flourish and start up your own greenhouse collection of greenery.

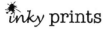

There are so many different things you can do in life, but rarely do we get the chance to actually do them, and then we forget all about them! So, here's a little bit of inspiration to get your mind going and give you some ideas for classes that you could go along to, giving you a taste and a try of something totally new, or just something old, forgotten, and left by the wayside – it's up to you.

1. Take a pottery class!
2. Try windsurfing
3. Or just plain surfing (!)
4. Go to a dance class
5. Get creative in the kitchen with a cookery class
6. Or, another course along the same lines… a cocktail-making or mixology or even wine-tasting class!
7. Go to a chocolate-making class and learn the history behind those delicious cocoa beans and the fine art of creating chocolate from bean!
8. Go to a life-drawing class

9. Get stretchy and flexy and go to a Pilates or yoga class

10. And relax with a meditation class

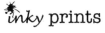

If you are still an active retiree, or looking to be more active in life, there are so many things that the outside world offers for you to try! Whether you're a beginner or at a higher level, going for gold standard, have a look at some of these active activities that you can try or get involved in doing.

1. Camping: a fun, simple, and often cheap holiday – whether you're tenting somewhere in the wilderness on your own, or renting a mobile home somewhere near the seaside, or taking a campervan / caravan off to your favourite campsite, camping can be so much fun and a great way to embrace the environment around you!

2. If walking is new to you, just try a short distance at a time, and gradually build it up. However, if you've done hiking before, challenge yourself and take a picnic for a full day of hiking, or maybe even a weekend of hiking somewhere like the New Forest of Peak District or Lake District! And if hiking really is your thing, why not take a true challenge and try the Three Peaks Challenge!?

3. Along the lines of doing something challenging –
   there are so many sporting challenges that you
   can get involved in and sign-up to so here are a
   few that you could think about doing:

   - 5k / 10k run for charity
   - Quarter marathon
   - Half marathon
   - Full marathon
   - Triathlon
   - Three Peaks
   - London to Brighton cycle ride
   - The colour run

4. Or, if you've never done sports before but are
   keen to get a bit more active, try taking up a new
   sport. Whether it's dancing with your partner, or
   tennis, golf, badminton, or even just some solo
   jogging… starting up and trying a new sport can
   be great in getting you active and also a nice new
   way to socialise.

5. Or if you would really just prefer getting active in
   a simple, safe way, why not go to a local gym for
   a workout?

6. Or the swimming pool at a local leisure centre?
   Joining as a member can offer you the option of
   going once a week or even every day for a nice

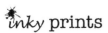

morning swim, and maybe even a sauna / steam, so that you're refreshed to start your day!

7. If pool-swimming isn't for you and you hate the chlorine, try some open water swimming – for example, in the Thames.

8. Cycling is currently something that is on the increase and that's being invested in. Plus, it's a great sport that can be done in the open air – or on an exercise bike machine inside – on both road or open country terrain. A cycle ride can be nice and leisurely, or part of a more intense training activity so whatever appeals to you, make it work and get active with your bicycle!

9. A sport that's a little more different but complete fun is skiing! If you've never skied before, it's a great thing to learn how to do and a wonderful way to spend a wintry holiday. If you have skied before and love doing so, why not try a new resort that you've always dreamed of skiing in? Or spend an entire ski-season on the slopes, now that time and work don't pose any restraints on your ability to do this!

10. Or, if skiing is not your thing, why not try snowboarding? Equally fun and with the same benefits as skiing, snowboarding is also a great

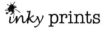

way to spend some of the wintry days that can otherwise seem so dark and dreary!

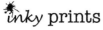

Treats come in all different shapes and sizes. Jars, filled with jam and marmalade, offer you a morning treat to spread on your toast. Yet how many people actually make their own? According to Statistica, in 2018, the UK sold 97.6 thousand tons of jam and jellies! So, why don't you try to make your own, for a change?

Here are ten different things you can get making, from jams to pickles to chutneys…

1. Plum and ginger jam
2. Basic blackberry jam
3. Mama's marmalade
4. Simple strawberry jam
5. Cox's apple chutney
6. Mincemeat
7. Lemon curd
8. Apple sauce
9. Tomato relish
10. Peanut butter

and a few of my favourite recipes to get you started…

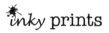

Plum and Ginger Jam

FROM NANA'S KITCHEN

You will need:

1kg ripe plums
1kg preserving sugar
1 tsp ground ginger
2 tsp lemon juice

How to:

Stone and quarter the plums.
Simmer plums in a pan for a few
minutes, until soft.
Sift in the ginger and add the
lemon juice.
Add sugar and stir until dissolved.
Bring to a boil and keep at a rolling
boil until setting point is reached
(around 30 mins).
Allow to cool for a few mins before
pouring into sterilised jars.

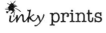
inky prints

Cox's Apple Chutney

FROM NANA'S KITCHEN

You will need:

7lb apples
2lb sultanas
1 onion
3lb brown sugar
1 tbsp crystallised ginger
1 tsp mixed spice
2pts vinegar
1 tsp cayenne pepper

How to:

Peel and chop the apples.
Add all the ingredients into
a big pan.
Boil until the sugar has
dissolved and then simmer
until it is thick.
Pour into sterilised jam jars
and let cool.

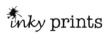

With additional time on your hands and skills to spare and share, why not do something for others to make a difference in the world? Retirement doesn't have to mean the end of the road for work and it's easy to volunteer in a local charity shop on a part-time basis, both keeping you busy and offering others a service for free. And why...? The answer is simple, giving offers you so much happiness and can bring an individual so much joy so dedicate some of your time in retirement to doing this and making a difference in the world.

1. Volunteer somewhere
2. Do something for charity
3. Fill a shoebox for Operation Christmas Child

Still not sure on what to put into your shoebox? Here's a few suggestions for you to consider…

WHAT TO PACK IN A CHRISTMAS SHOEBOX

- Toothbrush, flannel and soap
- A soft toy
- Pens, pencils, paper
- Hats and gloves and scarves
- Hairbrush / comb
- Friendship bracelet
- Purse / bag
- Toys - such as a yoyo, skipping rope, play-doh, doll
- Christmas card with well wishes

inky prints

4. Do a good deed for someone who is homeless

5. Complete a fundraiser

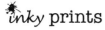 inky prints

Now that you're not restricted by time constraints, work, family, children… you're finally able to join the clubs that you've longed to join – whether that's a local darts club, or a swimming society, or the WI, or a book club with local residents… the world is your oyster.

If there's not a club that you've wanted to join, or something different you've wanted to try, take the social side element of being part of a club and build up your personal community and phonebook with some of the following clubs for inspiration:

1. Join a book club
2. Join the WI
3. Join a local community society
4. Form a dining club with friends
5. Join a social club

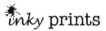

5 MORE WAYS TO…GET CREATIVE IN THE KITCHEN

Cooking and baking can be so therapeutic, calming, and whether or not it's something you've done before, it can be great fun to get creative in the kitchen. So, why not take on the challenge and cook a selection of the following:

1. Recreate a favourite dish you enjoyed during childhood… some classics might be savoury meals such as sausage, beans, and mash; or chicken nuggets and chips; or you might have a craving for something sweet such as jam tarts or a famous family recipe for chocolate cake!

2. After cooking an old childhood favourite, try to cook a new dish. Again, sweet or savoury, or both… there's plenty to try.

3. Cook an exotic dish from a foreign country that you've always wanted to go to….
   - Create pasta from scratch to mimic the stylish Italian cuisine

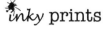 inky prints

- Or, if you prefer their pizza, mix up a pizza base and decorate it to your taste
- Stir up a hot Mexican: tacos, fajitas, burritos, quesadillas, or enchiladas and enjoy with salsa and guacamole!
- Another spicy dish you could try would be a hot Indian curry, or a Portuguese piri-piri!
- If you're really up for a challenge, you could try some creating a range of the Spanish Tapas dishes

4. Got lots of extra time? Why not bake some bread from scratch? From your basic white loaf to something different such as a soda or rye bread, or a loaf that offers a little more, such as a cheese and herb plait, or a garlic baguette, there's plenty to experiment with!

5. Or, if you prefer sweet bakery items, try making some pastry from scratch. There are five basic types of pastry that you can try: shortcrust, filo, choux, puff, and flaky pastry. Some are used for more savoury dishes: such as pies; others are perfect for making into buns or deserts.

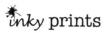 inky prints

Now that you're not limited to school holidays, or are not restricted by a certain number of holidays, or forced to go away only at weekends for a short break, the world is your oyster so make sure you maximise your chances and take plenty of trips!

Simple trips within your own country or exotic trips abroad, the choice is up to you!

1. Take a mini break in the middle of the week – just because you can!
2. Visit the place that you went to on your favourite childhood holiday – whether that's spending a day at Camber Sands or camping in Devon, or something overseas such as volunteering with elephants in Thailand or visiting Disney world, go and recreate that holiday once again. You could even take a few members of your family and make it a family holiday.
3. Visit somewhere you've always dreamed of going. Maybe that's going to Hawaii and swimming with some dolphins, or trekking across the Arctic circle,

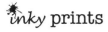

now's the best chance to travel and take the time to explore the place you've dreamed of visiting for years.

4. Visit a new country
5. Visit a new continent
6. Take a bus ride or train ride that includes beautiful sights that you can enjoy as you just gaze out of the window. Whether this is a train journey through the highlands in Scotland, or a bus trip around the sight-seeing destinations in London, or somewhere abroad, it's always great when you can sit back, relax, and enjoy the view.
7. Take a boating holiday. From barges to cruises, or sailing your own boat, spending time on the water can offer a new sort of tranquillity. There are so many options, depending on how much you want to spend and how active you're feeling...

- Renting a narrow boat and exploring networks of waterways, stopping off as you please to explore the shore
- Cruise off in style and luxury, with all inclusive food, drink, leisure and entertainment onboard, and the world to explore at any destination of your choice

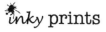

- Travel with a group on a holiday yacht and sail the seven seas in style
- Try an active holiday where you learn to sail, or similar
- Take a kayak or canoe and just have fun on the water

8. Take a break in the sunshine and work on your tan by catching those rays!

9. Take a wintry break. If you hate winter, you could always escape the colder season by taking a trip to a tropical resort during the winter months. Or, if you love winter, you can embrace the ice and snow thoroughly somewhere truly cold and snowy.

10. Take a city break to a capital city that you haven't yet visited and explore the typical tourist sites that everyone loves to go to, taking a selfie at every stop!

And, to help you plan and keep track of those trips…

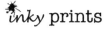

10 TRIPS I WANT TO TAKE...

1. _____

2. _____

3. _____

4. _____

5. _____

6. _____

7. _____

8. _____

9. _____

10. _____

10 THINGS TO…DO IN THE COMFORT OF YOUR OWN HOME

Now that you're not limited to school holidays, or are not restricted by a certain number of holidays, or forced to go away only at weekends for a short break, the world is your oyster so make sure you maximise your chances and take plenty of trips!

Simple trips within your own country or exotic trips abroad, the choice is up to you!

1. Re-read a favourite books series. Some popular ones include:
   - Harry Potter
   - Lord of the Rings
   - Anne of Green Gables
   - The Chronicles of Narnia
   - Malory Towers
   - His Dark Materials
   - Poldark
   - The Game of Thrones

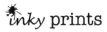

- The Da Vinci Code (Robert Langdon Series)
- Little House on the Prairie

2. Re-watch a series of movies. Some ideas to choose from might be:

    - Harry Potter
    - Lord of the Rings
    - Mission Impossible
    - The Dark Knight
    - Pirates of the Caribbean
    - Toy Story
    - James Bond
    - Ocean's
    - Shrek

3. Watch an entire box set. Netflix and other subscription services, such as Amazon Prime, make this really easy. Or you could watch it from a DVD if subscription services isn't for you.

4. Learn a new word from the dictionary every day – it's never too late to expand your vocabulary…

Hippopotomonstrosesquippedaliophobia - *one of the longest words in the dictionary. It is the name for a fear of long words, quite ironically!*[4]

---

[4]https://www.healthline.com/health/hippopotomonstrosesqui

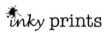

5. Read the newspaper with a nice cup of tea or coffee and a biscuit of your choice. Is it a 'rich tea' or a 'digestive'? A bourbon or custard cream for those who like biscuits that offer a little more… or a childhood party ring, jam tart, or jaffa cake (but is that a cake or a biscuit?!)

6. Sort through all your old photos and organise them into a format that you can enjoy looking at and sharing with others. It's lovely to be able to look back on photos taken during your childhood years, or on your wedding day, or at pivot moments during your life, or at moments that were simple yet perfectly sweet

7. While you're sorting out… sort out all your clothes – bin those that you've always kept 'just in case' and make yourself feel special by ensuring you have nice things to wear

8. Polish your shoes – a handy job to do but one that also makes you feel that little bit 'extra' when you get the chance to wear those shiny shoes at a later date!

9. Have a spring clean and clear out your cupboards, drawers, and maybe even your loft!

---

ppedaliophobia

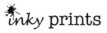 inky prints

10. Play a board game – for fun or for competition, games are a great way to unite everyone and entertain – especially if you have a large family and / or grandchildren too

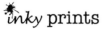

Quite often, when working, there is very little time for socialising or being around the people we value and care about. But retirement offers a whole new expanse of time that you can socialise in.

As well as having more time to socialise, there's more time to host and attend events. Whether it's a small gathering or a huge party, there's plenty of things that you can do with friends and family, such as

1. Hosting a Summer-time BBQ – why not invite around family, friends, neighbours, and members of the local community to enjoy some summer sunshine, relax with some drinks and nibbles, and socialise.
2. Have a night in with friends – whilst clubbing and going out all night partying might be in the past, there's no reason why you can't and shouldn't have friends around for a nnight-in. If it's beer and football, or wining and dining, or hot chocolate and a movie… whatever your preference, a night in with

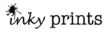 inky prints

friends can be whatever you make it and is a great way to enjoy yourself.

3. Go to a family party – families come in all shapes and sizes big, small, medium, extended, close… but no matter where in the world, it's nice for families to get together. A party poses the perfect opportunity to see each other and celebrate some family time.

4. Organise a surprise party – surprises come in all different shapes and sizes. Sometimes it's in the form of an unknown gift in a Christmas cracker, or a penny placed inside a piece of birthday cake… whatever form it comes in, a surprise can always make you smile. A surprise party gives you the chance to make someone else's day special so why not throw that special someone a surprise party – celebrating their birthday, anniversary, an achievement, or any event you fancy!

5. Invite your neighbours around for drinks and get to know those who live next door a little better.

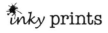

No more 'work days', but lots of spare days for different experiences and for doing a variety of new – or old and favourited – things. From having an extreme new experience, such as skydiving, to just repeating a familiar favourite experience, such as having a picnic with those you care about; there's plenty to do, whatever the weather.

1. Enjoy an afternoon tea somewhere nice (experiences to enjoy)
2. Treat yourself to a three-course meal
3. Go to the top of a tall building and see the view
4. Watch a show at the theatre
5. Have an indulgent spa day

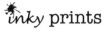

And finally, ... number 101…put your feet up and relax –
you've earned it!

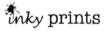

The retiree's
alphabet

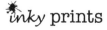

A

is for ADVENTURE

B

is for BREAKFAST IN BED

C

is for CELEBRATING LIFE

D

is for DIY

E

is for ENJOYMENT

F

is for FREEDOM

*inky prints

G

is for GRANDPARENT-HOOD

H

is for HOLIDAYS

I

is for INDEPENDENCE

J

is for JOY

K

is for KNOWLEDGE

L

is for LIVING LIFE TO THE FULL

M

is for MEMORIES

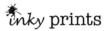

N

is for NEW EXPERIENCES

O

is for OPPORTUNITIES

P

is for PERSONAL TIME

Q

is for QUALITY OF LIFE

R

is for RELAXATION

S

is for SOCIALISING

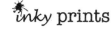

T

is for TRAVELLING

U

is for UNWINDING

V

is for VOLUNTEERING

W

is for WEEKDAYS

X

is for XTRA BONUSES / DISCOUNTS

Y

is for YOU-TIME

Z

is for ZEN

 inky prints

10 reasons to

retire

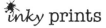

TOP TEN REASONS TO RETIRE

For some, retirement is an exciting opportunity and they can't wait to retire; however, for others, it's a dreaded step in life and perceived as the beginning of an end… So, just remind yourself of some great reasons to retire:

1. More free time to spend with family and friends
2. The opportunity to live your life to the full, and exactly how you want to
3. Improve your health by seizing the opportunity of exercising, having time to make and eat healthy meals, and relax more – destress!
4. Have the chance to pursue your passions and live your dreams to the max
5. A change to give back to your local community, to the world around you
6. Learn new and different things outside of the world of work
7. Move somewhere outside of the 'commuter zone' and enjoy a peaceful life in the countryside, by the sea, or up in the mountains
8. Escape the rat-race and daily routine and just have time to do as you please, whenever you please

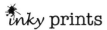 inky prints

9. Read all the books you've always wanted to read and watch all the movies you've always wanted to watch

10. Tick things off your bucket list!

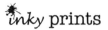 inky prints

Quotes to retire to

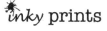

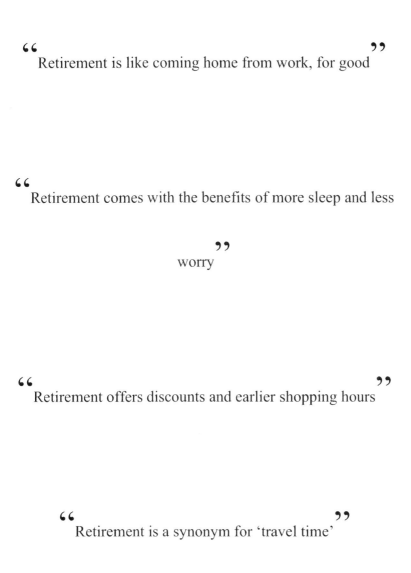

" Retirement is like coming home from work, for good "

" Retirement comes with the benefits of more sleep and less

" worry

" Retirement offers discounts and earlier shopping hours "

" Retirement is a synonym for 'travel time' "

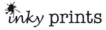

" "
Retirement is basically 'me time' made to sound fancy

" "
Retirement offers proof of hard work and perseverance

"
The trouble with retirement is that you never get a day

"
off   (*Abe Lemons*)

"   "
A retired husband is often a wife's full-time job   (*Ella*

Harris)

"Work is the curse of the drinking classes" (*Oscar*

Wilde)

"The best is yet to come!" (*Carolyn Leigh and Cy*

Coleman)

A limerick for retirement

 prints

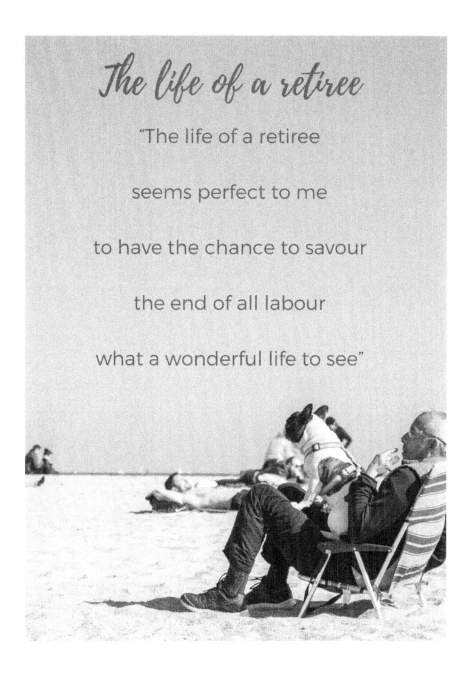

The life of a retiree

"The life of a retiree

seems perfect to me

to have the chance to savour

the end of all labour

what a wonderful life to see"

inky prints

Final words

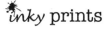

FINAL WORDS

Just remember… have a wonderful retirement – you've earned it!

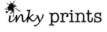

Printed in Great Britain
by Amazon

23878776R00047